GOD IS....

Copyright © 2019 Enger Lanier Taylor

All rights reserved. No part of this book may be used or reproduced, stored in a retrieval system or transmitted in any way by any means, electronic, mechanical, photocopy, recording or otherwise without the prior permission of the author.

Scripture quotations, unless otherwise indicated, are taken from the Holy Bible, King James Version.

Front Cover: D&K Productions
Back Cover: Enger Lanier Taylor – In Due Season Publishing LLC

Interior Designer:
Enger Lanier Taylor – In Due Season Publishing LLC

Published By: In Due Season Publishing, LLC
                    www.indueseasonpublishing.com
                    indueseasonpublishing@gmail.com

ISBN- 13: 978-0999238783

TABLE OF CONTENTS

INTRODUCTION 8

CHAPTER ONE 21

CHAPTER TWO 51

CHAPTER THREE 62

CHAPTER FOUR... 73

CHAPTER FIVE... 77

CHAPTER SIX.. 94

PROPHETIC ANNOUNCEMENTS 101

BIBLE VERSES
ABOUT THE AUTHOR

INTRODUCTION

One evening, I had a dream that someone was praying over my journal. The very next night, I had another dream, and I was given very specific details regarding this book, and what it should look like. This year I have been challenged in a variety of different ways, and most of the experiences were very unpleasant. But I thank God that He was, and continues to be with me every step of this journey. As I began to reflect on my entire life, I began to see more clearly how everything that has occurred has led me to this place. Hindsight is always 20/20.

At a very young age, my father killed himself. I would not understand the profound and significant impact that his actions would have in my life for many years to come. The trauma that I faced because of his actions was something that I did not even realize had taken place in my young mind, and heart. But a seed had been planted, which began to produce a harvest. Many of my thoughts, actions, and responses were viewed through the eyes of a rejected, abandoned, and wounded little girl who never felt like she was good enough. The enemy played tricks on my mind and told me, "Even your own daddy didn't love you enough to stay around." On the exterior, I may have been considered an accomplished young lady who excelled in school, held multiple pageant titles, and other extra-curricular activities. So, there were many years that I did what I thought others expected of me and what I thought that they needed me to be. Because my Heavenly Father is gracious and merciful, He saw me in my broken place and declared for me to "live." I had no idea that I was drowning. I was too busy pretending to be "fine," when I was crumbling. For many years I struggled with knowing my true value and worth. I could not see myself as My Heavenly Father saw me.

Years ago, I had a dream, where I saw my face and written across my forehead was the word ENCOURAGER. From that point, I knew that no matter what may be going on in my personal life, that God had given me a voice. One of the ways that He wanted me to use it was to speak to the discouraged, brokenhearted, lonely, disgusted and traumatized. I must let them know that they can accomplish what our Father has ordained for them to do. No matter what their life may look like presently; He loves them.

There are many facets to our Father; He is everything that we need. At every season in our lives, we will be faced with challenges, setbacks, joys, heartbreak. Life is full of highs and lows. However, we have many promises of God. Every promise He has given is up to us to receive. My prayer for you is that this book will challenge you to look at everything in your life that has kept you from living a full, purposeful life where God can use your transparency to help other people. No longer should we be looking for platforms, accolades, acceptance and the applause of others when we should be living our lives for the applause of "ONE." Our focus should be on our creator. People will come and go, but God remains the same. He never changes. God Is.

On the days that I began to write this book something profound happened. My prayer often has been, "God, please reveal to me anything in my heart that is not pleasing to you or that is keeping me from moving forward." I had been feeling stuck. I had

GOD IS....

come through a tough series of challenges and while God was expanding, developing and correcting some things in my life; He seemed to be catapulting and shifting me for the better all at the same time. Even as I write this, I feel as if I am in a very strange and uncomfortable season but still full of expectation and excitement. Oftentimes, I have spent a lot of time and energy, pushing others to where I knew that God had declared for their lives. I have come to understand that I am adamant about pushing others and helping to make sure that they complete their tasks. In the past, I neglected the very assignments and giftings that God placed inside of me. I have been much more comfortable being in the background when that was only one part of my purpose.

Dreams and prophetic words that had been spoken over my life 10-20 years ago are starting to manifest. Before maturing, I would frequently revisit those words, I would wonder if I heard God correctly, or was it just my own imagination. But I knew that the things that He had shown me were far beyond anything that I could have dreamed of for myself. The how, what, when and where secrets that only God knew. Only He knew the pain, rejection, bitterness, abandonment, loneliness, and struggle that had to be dug out so that

I could be a vessel of honor.

I am not concerned about how many gifts you have. The gifts of God are just that, "gifts" and He will give them to whomever He chooses. People can be gifted and have no character, integrity, or represent the Kingdom of God well. If we are to represent our Father, we must look like Him.

We can't spend so much time focusing on someone else's journey and neglect our own. While you may have watched other people promoted, acknowledged, and platformed, the work that needs to be done on you has gone undone. I absolutely celebrate my brothers and sisters as they fulfill their assignments in God, and I am not jealous of their accomplishments. Every one of us has individual tasks and destinies and all our journeys are different. If some of these people would share their real testimonies, you would not be as quick to wish you were who you think that they are. Many of you have been rejected, abused and left for dead by the enemy. But just like Joseph, who was thrown into a pit and sold into slavery, by those that were supposed to care for and love him he overcame the odds and delivered the same people who hurt him. His journey was not easy, and he suffered many setbacks, but God used every situation and elevated him to a position of honor when it was his "due season." So, don't think for one moment that these great prophetic words that you have received are not going to be opposed by the adversary, because they will. In the back of this book, you will be encouraged to document those prophetic words that have been spoken over your life, so you learn how to 'war' on their behalf. There will be a time that you will need to consistently rehearse them in your own hearing so that you do not forget what God said. You must remember that it is during these seasons when you feel like you want to give up and throw in the towel that you must continue to move forward realizing that everything you need is in God. He will never allow you to be overloaded or overwhelmed, but you must put your complete trust and reliance in Him.

My prayer for you is that while you read and work through this book that you will be challenged to take a deep look at yourself and allow the Holy Spirit to root out all the things that are in your soul that has caused you to be wounded, hard-hearted, rebellious, and envious. You will even become aware of some behavior and addictions that are common in your bloodline that need to be destroyed so that the next generation will not be hindered for walking in their destiny.

Don't keep pretending that you are fine when you know that you must be rescued by a loving Father. There is no need to continue to hide from others. Your testimony can set the captives free and help others to be an overcomer. The enemy would want you to be ashamed of your past so that you won't share your pain and all that you have been through. Trust me; I have often said, "Every smiling face ain't happy." Many people pretend to be something that they are not. Life's circumstances have caused many to be depressed and locked into a life of never-ending cycles that don't seem to end. Jesus came that we might have an abundant life but first, we must deal with our soul (mind, will, and emotions). Transparency is vital because others need to know that they are not alone in their struggle.

While reading this book you will also have an opportunity to write your own "Letter to God." By doing so you will realize that there may be some unresolved issues in your heart that have kept you from moving forward. You may find that there are people who you have not forgiven and how this has possibly affected your current relationships. Nothing is off limits. Let's be real so that we can heal. As you begin, you probably will be surprised as to what comes out of your heart. Our heart is desperately wicked, who can know it (Jeremiah 17:9)? Grab your pen and allow the Holy Spirit to go deep and reveal the things that have been holding you back. The beginning of this process is to first acknowledge that there is work that must be done and you must submit yourself. It will not be easy, but it will be worth it.

This book is going to release you to acknowledge that we all have had terrible things that have happened to us in our lives. Nevertheless, in order for us to move up and onward, we must be inwardly healed. God has been and *God Is* your healer, defense, protector, strength, strong tower, deliverer and a multitude of other names that you will be encouraged to write and reflect on. Allow this book to remind you that as the eagle, you can use the wind of every storm to rise above every setback and set up so that you can soar and teach others to do the same.

Some of your prophetic words and dreams will carry very specific instructions that you will need to remember and act upon. Also, there will be times that you will need to revisit them and remind yourself of what God has ordained for your life and put Him in remembrance of His Word. It is not that He has forgotten, but so when your adversary attempts to cause you to believe his lies, you are continually reminded that God's declarations and decrees shall manifest, but you must war on behalf of those promises.

There is no set time of completion. Your process will be determined by your willingness to submit and obey whatever God has shown you that must be destroyed. Simply put; you must die! Your opinions must die! Your attitudes must die and your right to be right must die! Let's Go….

GOD IS....

As you begin to write this letter to God, you may be very uncomfortable. You may be saying, "God knows everything, so why do I need to write Him a letter?" Sometimes, when you are writing, there is a freedom that comes with every stroke of the pen. You can rid yourself of all the anxiety, pain, and the many questions that you may have. There is no right or wrong way to begin. Just pour out your heart and be completely naked before your Father. Confession is good for the soul.

Dear God,

_____
_____
_____
_____
_____
_____
_____
_____
_____
_____
_____
_____
_____
_____
_____
_____
_____
_____
_____
_____

ENGER LANIER TAYLOR

GOD IS....

ENGER LANIER TAYLOR

CHAPTER ONE

Comforter

Webster defines rejection as being cast aside, or refusal to accept. At one point, we have felt as if we were cast aside, or we have been the one who has pushed people away. Some of our earliest feelings of being shunned have occurred in childhood. These experiences have oftentimes been etched in our brains and followed us through to our adult lives. Many relationships may have suffered because of what has happened in our past. We have a lifetime full of those memories that have shaped some of our attitudes, and behaviors regarding who we are, and our perception of what other people think of us. From the time we are born, we are looking for ways to avoid pain. Instead of facing those uncomfortable thoughts, we might take mental detours. Deep emotional pain can also manifest as physical ailments. Early in life, we learn what attitudes will gain responses to get what we need or want. As infants and toddlers, we may have learned that having a temper tantrum got us what we wanted. We learn to manipulate people without realizing that is what we are doing.

What does a person do with the emotions of being disappointed, hurt, shunned, rejected, and abandoned? I did as many other people do; I stuffed those emotions for many years. For me, brick by brick I began to build a wall, and hide behind a manufactured smile to fool people. No one knew how much I was hurting, and neither did I. I became very good at building walls. The only thing was, I could not get out, and I was not letting anyone else in.

As young as five years old, I began to build myself a wall. My whole world came tumbling down when my father killed himself. My father's funeral was the first that I could remember ever attending. I had no concept of death or what it meant. All I knew was that the man that I adored was lying very still and did not respond to my inward pleas to wake up. Like most little girls, my father always seemed to be very strong and courageous. I don't remember us doing anything extraordinary. However, I do remember him carrying me around his neck and walking me to my grandmother's house. On another occasion one summer afternoon we laid on a blanket in my grandmother's back yard staring up at all the clouds. From what I later came to learn about him from one of his best friends that he was a deep thinker who I simply adored. Without knowing it, when my husband and I purchased our first home God orchestrated that home be right next door to that very same best friend who was able to tell me a lot of things about my dad that I did not know. I was so thankful that God loved me enough to send me to that street so that my father's best friend was able to watch our two sons grow up, take them fishing and tell them stories about their grandfather. As I got older, I felt like I had been robbed, although I had no idea of all the things that had been stolen.

All my life, there was a longing inside me that I could never express. Later, I really began to sincerely seek a closer relationship with God, and continually asked Him questions during my prayer time like, "What is hindering me from having a closer walk with you and Why does there seem to be a brick wall that keeps me from coming closers." One day, while I was looking out of my window at work, and just thinking about how good God had been to me, I heard a small voice say, "You are angry with your father." Initially, I thought that was ridiculous because I loved him so much. But the more I sat and pondered, I knew that it was true. I had been angry for so many years because my father had made a choice that affected not just me, my mom, his mother or his siblings, but his grandchildren. A torrential downpour of tears was released at the mere admission of my anger and deep sadness. I grieved for the first time in my life for my father. How could this be? At that time, I was around thirty years old. It had taken me about twenty-five years to 'begin' to grieve. It was as if he had just died. It was hard to believe that after all those years the pain could be so fresh. I grieved for our lost relationship and the fact that he would never get to know his grandchildren.

During this time, I encountered the true grace of God. For me, the "death walk" had begun. I felt like I was dying, and I could not stop the process. The

> *Job 5:17*
> Behold, happy is the man who God corrects, therefore do not despise the chastening of the Almighty.

truth of it is I was getting exactly what I asked for. I wanted to be like God in character and there were some old dead issues that had to be brought to the surface so they could be dealt with. My desire to be more like God was stronger than my desire to hold on any longer to things that were only going to keep me out of His presence, such as anger. Do not waste precious time. Just say yes to the will and purpose that God has established for your life and every area even when it hurts. If your heart's desire is to grow and mature in your spiritual walk, you must be able to receive correction from Him. Your response to what He says is going to truly let you know where you really are and not where you 'think' you are.

I had to forgive my father and I had to forgive myself. It became clearer for me to understand some of the blockages that I had in my life regarding relationships. I began to question every relationship that I had. Had I been guarding my heart so closely that I did not let in the people that I needed the most? The deeper I looked, the more I realized that there were probably other relationships that had suffered because I did not allow myself to fully trust. As Holy Spirit began to minister to me, He explained to me that my father had said he loved me and then left me. Therefore, I was apprehensive about trusting God who I could not see when in my mind, I could not trust the father that I could see. We tend to treat our Heavenly Father a lot like our earthly fathers. So, if those earthly fathers abused our trust, neglected us and never made us feel safe, then our relationships with God probably suffered without us even being aware of it. Unknowingly, after the death of my father a part of me shut down. Although, I loved God, a part of me did not completely trust Him. Why? I was afraid to let go and give my life and everything that I thought that meant. I had been let down and abandoned by the man who said he loved me which led me to have unrealistic expectations of others. No one will ever be able to affirm or love you like the one who created you.

We must understand that to deal with the issues we can no longer just deal with the result of our actions or feelings. We must deal with the root of the problem. We want the seed of the thing that we are dealing with to be uprooted completely. Otherwise, we will continually be dealing with the same circumstances. How many times have you thought that you have dealt with something only to find out through the pressures of life that you had only covered it up for it to resurface later?

Someone Else Needs Access

Some years ago, we had two sizable pine trees in our front yard, which were terrible to maintain and causing damage to our roof. So, we decided to cut them down. At some point, a little squirrel must have buried a seed and another tree began to grow right in the middle of my flower bed. Since I was not familiar with types of plants and trees, I would just cut the top off as far as possible. Of course, it would continue to grow, and I would continue to trim. It was getting to be a little aggravating. This ugly thing always seemed to appear right after I had trimmed the hedges and pruned the flowers.

One day my next door neighbor, who was my father's best friend, was talking to me on my front porch and pointed out what was happening in my flower bed. He instructed me that even though I was trimming the top of the tree, the roots were continuing to grow and could cause some major damage to my pipes since it was so close to the house if it were not dug up by the root. How many times have you been putting on a smile and filling your life with busy work just to cover up what was really going on underneath? You just continued to pretend that all was well in your world when truthfully, something was threatening the very core of your existence.

He continued that the ground was very dry and that I would have to wait until it had rained so the soil would be soft, which would make the job of digging the tree up by the root much easier. Have you allowed your heart to become so hard that the roots of bitterness don't have a chance of being pulled up? That is exactly what goes on in our lives. We allow life circumstances and pain to govern our emotions and we attempt to hide behind layers of pain, and we become hard.

One day after a heavy rain, I took a shovel and began the attempt to dig up the root of what was causing the trouble. The work proved to be too hard for me, so I called for my husband to come to the rescue with more muscle power. As suspected, the roots were much deeper and more spread out than I thought. All of this had taken place underground, where I did not see the potential damage that could have taken place. While I had been cutting off what I could see on the surface, the roots were continuing to grow out of sight. That is what has occurred in many of our lives. How many times have we noticed behaviors and situations that seem to continually pop up and we believe that we have dealt with the issue at hand until it occurs again? Sometimes life's circumstances cause our hearts to harden, which is exactly what the enemy wants you to do. He wants you to lose hope and faith in God. While the surface may look perfect, there are things that we have refused to deal with or even realized would affect us and would inevitably begin to cause trouble. We may look all put together on the outside, but on the inside, some of us are all messed up.

First, I had to admit that there was a problem. I had to bathe my situation with prayer. Then, there had to be an identification of what I was dealing with. Lastly, a course of action had to be determined. Even after realizing that the tree had to be dug up, I knew that it could not be uprooted at the time that it was identified. Why not? The ground was very dry. Just because we acknowledge that we have a situation that needs the healing touch of our Heavenly Father, does not mean that healing comes immediately. Even when we are sick, we understand that there is a process before complete healing is manifested. Our spiritual life is much the same in that every person must go through their own individual process. So, it is very unwise to compare your life to another because you have no idea what issues they have had to deal with. People seem to want the gifts that God gave someone else, not understanding that they had to be processed to that place. Every anointing has an assignment and a specific crushing that goes along with it. Never envy another person's anointing. You have no idea what they had to endure for the oil to flow. The grass always seems to be greener on the other side. It only looks that way until you get to the other side and find out that there are weeds over there too and you must dig them up if you want the lawn to meet your expectations.

You must be willing to:
- Evaluate yourself
- Admit there is a problem
- Allow the Holy Spirit to identify the problem
- Address the situation
- Do not be afraid of seeing what is wrong with you
- Don't waste time feeling sorry for yourself

Our attitude during trials must be one that holds on to the faithfulness of our Lord and Savior Jesus Christ. Anytime, we are going through life challenges we must understand that God wants us to totally rely on Him and not ourselves. The good news is that God comforts us in our tribulation. However, He does not tell us when, where or how that comfort will manifest in our lives. The Word declares that weeping may endure for a night, but He did not tell us how long our "night" would last. The promise is that joy comes in the morning. We must stop looking at the setbacks of life as something that was designed to take us out. The enemy may have had a plan to kill, steal and destroy, but God's plans will always prevail over what the enemy desires to do in your life.

Even when God has comforted us in our affliction, we should readily be available to share and comfort, encourage and uplift those who may find themselves in similar circumstances. It sometimes baffles me to see how many of us claim to have been delivered but refrain from being any assistance to those that we know are struggling, despondent and hopeless. For so many, shame has kept us from sharing our stories and revealing some of the most intimate parts of our lives.

<u>2 Corinthians 1:3-7(KJV)</u>	<u>2 Corinthians 1:3-7 (Message)</u>
³ Blessed be God, even the Father of our Lord Jesus Christ, the Father of mercies, and the God of all comfort; ⁴ Who comforteth us in all our tribulation, that we may be able to comfort them which are in any trouble,	3-5 All praise to the God and Father of our Master, Jesus the Messiah! Father of all mercy! God of all healing counsel! He comes alongside us when we go through hard times, and before you know it, he brings us alongside someone else who is

by the comfort wherewith we ourselves are comforted of God.

⁵ For as the sufferings of Christ abound in us, so our consolation also aboundeth by Christ.

⁶ And whether we be afflicted, it is for your consolation and salvation, which is effectual in the enduring of the same sufferings which we also suffer: or whether we be comforted, it is for your consolation and salvation.

⁷ And our hope of you is steadfast, knowing, that as ye are partakers of the sufferings, so shall ye be also of the consolation.

1 Peter 5:9-11 (KJV)

⁹ Whom resist steadfast in the faith, knowing that the same afflictions are accomplished in your brethren that are in the world.

¹⁰ But the God of all grace, who hath called us unto his eternal glory by Christ Jesus, after that ye have suffered a while, make you perfect, stablish, strengthen, settle you.

¹¹ To him be glory and dominion forever and ever. Amen.

going through hard times so that we can be there for that person just as God was there for us. We have plenty of hard times that come from following the Messiah, but no more so than the good times of his healing comfort—we get a full measure of that, too.

6-7 When we suffer for Jesus, it works out for your healing and salvation. If we are treated well, given a helping hand and encouraging word, that also works to your benefit, spurring you on, face forward, unflinching. Your hard times are also our hard times. When we see that you're just as willing to endure the hard times as to enjoy the good times, we know you're going to make it, no doubt about it.

1 Peter 5:9-11 (Message)

8-11 Keep a cool head. Stay alert. The Devil is poised to pounce and would like nothing better than to catch you napping. Keep your guard up. You're not the only ones plunged into these hard times. It's the same with Christians all over the world. So, keep a firm grip on the faith. The suffering won't last forever. It won't be long before this generous God who has great plans for us in Christ—eternal and glorious plans they are!—will have you put together and on your feet for good. He gets the last word; yes, he does.

GOD IS....

Our lessons seem to be never ending and seem to increase when we are going through. What all this suffering and despair may produce in you is greater compassion for those who are also going through seasons of trials and tests. The good news is that God Himself will strengthen, establish, perfect and make your footsteps firm so that you do not slip. God is making you into His image and it is not always comfortable or pain free.

When gold is being processed, it is placed in a fire that causes the impurities to float to the surface. That is one of the reasons we may begin to see all kinds of character flaws that come to the surface when we are going through tough times. We may not know what is in us until the pressure is placed on us. God allows us to see those things that were hidden in order that we might better understand that He desires pure vessels. Therefore, we should not be surprised when we go through fiery trials, as though we should be exempt from them. They are not meant to kill you but perfect you.

Indeed, suffering may come because we are living a godly life. We may suffer physically, psychologically and emotionally, but we must remember that we have a High Priest who knows the feeling of our infirmities. Many people are interested in knowing Christ only in the power of His resurrection. But few are willing to fellowship in His sufferings. Like Jesus, we are to learn obedience through the things that we suffer (Hebrews 5:8). Did you catch that? We learn. Suffering is a school that has many lessons to offer and we are graded by our responses.

What is your typical or first response when something occurs in your life? It can be said of many, that we may run to other people instead of running to God for safety, security, and counsel. Why? Although God has proven Himself continually to be faithful, sometimes we have shown ourselves not to rely on the one who created, established, redeemed and kept us. We get ourselves into trouble when we seek everyone and everything else before seeking God when He should be our first and not last resort. We seem to have things backward. I do believe that all of us should have friends that we can confide in but at no time should we seek their counsel and instruction above the Word of God.

GOD IS....

GOD IS... *A Comforter*

Write down your personal experiences where God revealed Himself to you as a comforter. How do you plan to help share the comfort that God has given you with others?

> **_John 14:16 KJV_**
> *And I will pray the Father, and He shall give you another comforter that He may abide with you forever.*

> **_John 15:26 KJV_**
> *But when the comforter is come, whom I will send unto you for the Father, even the spirit of truth which proceedeth from the Father, he shall testify of me.*

Remember the times that you were in a situation where you needed the comfort of the Holy Spirit. Write at least three (3) things where God brought you through a difficult time. This will help you remember that God is the same yesterday, today and forever. Even though you may be dealing with a tragedy, disappointment, and discouragement, remember that the same comfort that you have received is what you need to extend to others.

Meditating on God's Word should always bring us comfort; whether it is for correction, assurance, love, care, correction or direction. Help can be found for every situation that we may find ourselves in.

1._____
2._____
3._____

Days of Adversity

Whatever may be happening is only for a moment in time. No one knows or can say how long that "moment" will last. Keep holding on and go through this period of purification and purging. You can make it! I know you may feel as if you can't take anymore and you want to throw in the towel. You can't give up now.

Whatever you do; don't faint. While you maneuver through your season of affliction, it is very important that you remember that whatever "trouble" you may encounter; whether it is emotional, physical or spiritual that Paul says that these are light afflictions. Paul states that our light affliction is but for a moment and is working for us a far more exceeding eternal weight of glory (2 Cor. 4:17).

Adversity is a state of hardship or affliction. We have all gone through or are going through some hardships. The American Heritage Dictionary defines the word *faint* as lacking strength, conviction, courage or boldness. When we are afflicted by life's hard blows or suffering hardships, our lack of ability to be bold and courageous means that we have little strength (Proverbs 24:10).

When training for any sort of event, it would be highly unlikely that an athlete could expect to win without training. They are usually paying special attention to their diet. There is weightlifting and critiquing by a coach who is monitoring their progress. We will have a test, trial or setback for the battle ahead. The time to prepare for hardship is before we get to that point. That is why we must read, study and pray diligently always because we don't know when life is going to deal hardships. If we have prepared for those times beforehand, we will not be weak and timid, because we have not filled ourselves with what we need in order to endure.

Foundation

Part of my background is in the real estate and construction industry. I love how God will use your natural occupation and give spiritual context. Naturally speaking, before anything can be built, proper procedures must be followed to make sure that what is being built will not fall. Once the desired location of the building has been identified, typically one will need to employ the services of a geotechnical engineer who will be able to determine if the soil is the composition that it should be for the foundation to be laid. That's right; you cannot just go out and put a foundation on top of soil which has not been tested. The soil composition of different parts of the country and sometimes even in the same city is not the same. In cases where the soil has too much sand in it, which would be considered unsuitable soils, must be dug out and replaced and compacted with soil that is considered suitable.

Everything that we may be going through is nothing compared to what is going to be revealed in us. If something is revealed that means that at one time or another, it was covered up. God is going to pull back the layers like an onion and show people that while you were hidden, beneath the surface He was doing surgery on you in secret. He did not expose us to the world while He was working on us behind closed doors and let the world see our dysfunction. But instead, He was cutting out things that did not belong and putting things in that would give Him glory.

We are being treated much like diamonds, which are created deep beneath the earth under intense heat and pressure. So, if this describes your current state, know that God is shaping you into a diamond. However, that is just the beginning. After the diamond is located and extracted, that is when the real work begins. The diamond must be cut and polished so that the true beauty of it can be revealed. Since the diamond is the hardest natural substance another diamond must be used to cut it. The primary object of diamond cutting is to bring out the fire and brilliance of the stone. Equally important is the cutting of the stone according to a plan that will eliminate imperfections, such as cracks, flaws and cloudiness and will produce a gem of the greatest size, best appearance, and maximum value. So, God has a master plan for the imperfections and flaws to be taken out of our lives. It requires some cutting and polishing to acquire the finished product which is a magnificent diamond.

I remember when the cubic zirconia was first introduced to the jewelry market. To the untrained eye, they looked just like the real thing. Through the years they have been made so well that unless the person that is looking at them is a gem expert, one might not be able to tell the difference between the real and the fake. Both look the same on the outside, but once they are more closely inspected with a magnifier, the truth is revealed.

Do not worry about what other people look like on the outside. Some people you may look at seem like they have it all together. Oftentimes, we have looked at them and admired their "beauty." They may look like the real thing, but upon closer examination by the Master Diamond Cutter, which is Holy Spirit, what we thought was a priceless diamond is only a cheap imitation. Do not get caught up on what it looks like God is doing in the life of someone else. You really do not know what is going on behind closed doors. The only person you need to be concerned with is yourself and the process that God has you in right now.

To be concerned and sidetracked with what is going on in the lives of other people in respect to who we think are spiritual giants is a big waste of time and is a trick of the enemy to get us off focus. Stay focused, no matter what because if you are not careful, you can miss some very important lessons.

Holy Spirit instructed me to write this book in twenty-one days. Shortly afterward, our family experienced the death of my stepfather. My point is, no matter what is going on in your life. You must remember that God knew what would be going on in and around you before He gave you your assignment and He still requires that you finish it. I pray that the "yes" that you gave God did not have conditions attached to it. You must know that you will be tested and tried for every word you gave back to God. If you said, "God, I trust you." You probably are going to be in some situations that are going to test your level of faith. At that point, you may recognize that you don't trust him at the level you thought you did.

Strengthen Your Relationship

I challenge you to not only seek the face of God when you are in trouble but have an ongoing relationship with Him. Holy Spirit was given for instruction and guidance and He is our comforter. To be able to receive this instruction that we so desperately need, we must be in fellowship with Him, because He is always willing to assist us.

What would you think about a child, a spouse or a friend who would only call you when they were in a tight situation and needed some help? You would soon grow weary of their phone calls. What would your reaction be to someone who called often but wanted nothing except to tell you how much they loved you, respected you and just wanted to spend time with you? Can you imagine what our Heavenly Father would do for those who just seek to love Him? I want you to seriously consider something. Everything that has happened and will happen to all of us is nothing in the big scheme of things. Jesus was talked about, ostracized, criticized, lied on and crucified by men when He had laid down His life for them. You may feel hopeless, misunderstood and rejected but hold on sisters and brothers; wipe those tears and stop the pity party. Tears do not move God. He is moved by your faith.

As I was saying earlier, Holy Spirit gave me a deadline in which this book was to be completed, which was twenty-one days, all while I was in the midst of working my full-time job, working with other authors to publish their books, showing houses as a real estate agent and ministering. God already knew what would transpire in those days. As I began to write, I wondered why the very first attribute that I wrote was "Comforter." Little did I realize that He already saw where my journey would take me. A few days after He gave me this mandate, On August 6, 2017, my stepfather was called home to be with the Lord. He endured many years of suffering in his body. Both of his kidneys had been removed; both of his legs had been amputated; he was a dialysis patient; high blood pressure; heart problems and had broken his neck in earlier years while he was still working. But even with all those ailments, setbacks and disappointments, he continued to travel, preach, conduct Bible studies and go about his life as normally as possible.

When I got the news, my mind was filled with who needed to be notified, emotionally supported and all sorts of things that needed to be taken care of. It is typical of me to think about everyone else and not consider my own emotional needs. While I was sitting on the couch trying to gather my thoughts, Holy Spirit reminded me of what His instructions were to me. The book <u>must</u> be written in 21 days and seven days had already gone by with planning the funeral. I sat there baffled at the thought and held my head down because I knew exactly what He was saying. God already knew what was coming before He gave me the directions. I could not offer any excuses. I knew that whatever was going on in my personal life, He was giving me the grace I needed to do what He mandated. Don't ever allow "life" to keep you from obeying God. He knows the end from the beginning. Oftentimes, we give God a fresh, "Yes," and soon thereafter, all hell seems to break loose. This should never be a surprise. Why? The enemy wants to kill, steal and destroy your destiny and purpose. He will typically use the same tricks that he used to distract you in the past. Whether he is attempting to cause chaos in your family, on your job, with your children or in your health. He does not want you to fulfill what God has preordained for your life. Our lives are not our own and we were created to influence others. If he can distract you and cause you not to finish your assignment, there will be others who will suffer from your disobedience.

There have been several times when I was met with opposition and adversity when I was moving forward to complete an assignment. Unfortunately, there were many times that the blows I received caused me to draw back or be consumed with my situation instead of staying focused on the One who gives me comfort and strength during those times. Consistently, I have cried out to God.

Sometimes not realizing that it was during some of my darkest hours that my reliance on Him alone is where I noticed the most spiritual growth. During seasons of my deepest pain and despair, He heard my cry.

    Like many of you, I have depended on myself when I should have been leaning and trusting in my Lord and Savior for everything that I needed. But I looked to myself and others to fill needs that they were not equipped to meet, which only left me feeling abandoned and rejected. I had unrealistic expectations of people who were broken just like me. They were in no position to help me because they did not know that they needed help themselves. Ecclesiastes said it best when it came to chronicle the ups and downs of life. Even with the cycles, you may endure, you can be confident that He has never left you. Though there may be heartbreak and pain; there will also be joy and laughter.

Seasons

- To everything there is a season and a time to every purpose under the heaven;
- A time to be born and a time to die; a time to plant and a time to pluck up that which is planted;
- A time to kill and a time to heal, a time to break down and a time to build up;
- A time to weep, and a time to laugh; a time to gather stones together; a time to embrace and a time to refrain from embracing;
- A time to get and a time to lose; a time to keep and a time to cast away;
- A time to rend and a time to sew; a time to keep silence and a time to speak;
- A time to love and a time to hate; a time of war and a time of peace;

I will tell you now that although you may be in the valley, the assignments and tasks that you have been given to you still must be completed and you can do it. Surely, you did not think that the enemy was going to stop opposing the plan of God for your life. Do not faint or grow weary during this storm. Take a deep breath and refocus. Far too often, we take our eyes off God and put them on the promise, which will leave you feeling despondent and exasperated. You are being stretched so that you can endure the hardships of life. Be aware that your transparency and testimony will enable others who may feel as if they have no hope to see that they too can overcome anything that the enemy tries to use to distract them and throw them off course.

What/Who have you allowed to distract you and keep you from pursuing and completing your God-assignment?

_____
_____
_____
_____
_____
_____
_____
_____
_____
_____
_____
_____
_____
_____

GOD IS....

What will you do to ensure that you are not placing other's opinions above what God has told you to do?

ENGER LANIER TAYLOR

2

CHAPTER TWO

Adversity Leads to Self-Examination

At times God will allow adverse situations to touch all our lives. Adversity is an opportunity for us to examine what is truly in our hearts. Typically, we do not truly know what is in us until there is external psychological and/or spiritual pressure applied. Inevitably, who we really are will show up at some point. Although no one likes to be put in situations where our "ugliness" is revealed, there are opportunities for us to examine ourselves. Without adversity, you may be deceived into thinking that you are just fine, and something is wrong with everyone else.

We should be examining ourselves regularly. Paul encouraged

the Corinthians, "Let a man examine himself" (1 Cor. 11:28). In other words, "Take an inquisitive look inside and discover what is driving, motivating and enticing you. (Charles Stanley- Advancing Through Adversity pg. 36). God does not desire that our negative life experiences fester in our hearts and bitterness and offense to defile others. We (Christians) are the temple of the Holy Spirit and our temples should be clean and useable vessels. We should be free from our memories, unresolved issues, and unreconciled relationships. We cannot allow those issues to go unresolved. As with trees whose roots grow deep, if we do not deal with our "issues" then those roots are harder to excavate and dig up.

Unforgiveness is a vice that is tormenting the masses. I am not speaking of those outside the church, but among those who profess to be saved. I have seen and known far too many of us who have been "in the church" for 10, 15, 20 or more years and won't talk to their spiritual or natural brothers or sisters because they have been offended. People, our hearts must be examined consistently. The more I listen to some "saved" people the more my heart breaks. Without asking any questions, you can soon determine the issues of their soul. We can't shout and dance over offense and think that we are validated in our responses to other people's actions. You cannot control how people treat you or perceive you. However, you are in control of how you respond to them. You may have been legitimately wronged but responding with evil is never the answer and it is not God's way of doing things.

At this point, you may recognize that you need a "heart check." Typically, we go to the doctor for a physical checkup yearly to make sure that there isn't anything going on that needs to be monitored further. The same cannot or should not be said about our spiritual hearts. We are daily met with opportunities to be offended, wounded, angry or bitter. When we take note that the enemy is attempting to place these seeds in our hearts, we must promptly deal with them. You should never allow the lies of the enemy to potentially cut off your fellowship with the Father, which is exactly what your adversary desires to do.

Can you identify with the following questions or comments?

1. I wouldn't have acted that way if they had not done this to me.
2. I am never talking to them again because they hurt my feelings.
3. I may forgive them, but I will never forget what they did.

4. Who do they think they are anyway? I remember when they did....
5. The Lord knows my heart. *He sure does and He wants you to submit yourself to Him so you can receive a heart transplant.*

If so, you need to meditate and ponder on these scriptures.

The Spirit of the man is the lamp of the Lord, searching all the inner depths of his heart **(Proverbs 20:27)**.

Let us search out and examine our ways and turn back to the Lord; Let us lift our hearts and hands to God in heaven **(Lamentations 3:40-41)**.

Search me, O God and know my heart; Try me and know my anxieties, and see if there is any wicked way in me; and lead me in the way everlasting **(Psalm 139: 23-24)**.

The heart is deceitful above all things and desperately wicked, who can know it? **(Jeremiah 17:9)**.

Deal with It

Some people have found themselves in abusive relationships and eventually found the strength to leave. They tend to carry some heavy baggage into other relationships and sometimes become very defensive. They may have been in an abusive relationship with Fred and divorced him. But because they have not been healed from the relationship with Fred when Danny comes along, they still remember all the things that Fred did to them and Danny ends up suffering the consequences for it. Poor Danny is in competition with someone that he probably has never laid eyes on before. In the mind of a woman who has finally gotten the courage to leave an abusive relationship, whether it is physical or emotional, she is sure to say, "I will never let another man do what Fred did to me again!" In essence, Danny has a hard time gaining his wife's trust. She is so wounded that she has placed an emotional barricade around herself. Past hurts and pains, whether they have come from ex-husbands, friends, family members or acquaintances gone unchecked can ruin potential friendships that God may be sending your way.

Root causes of pain and heartache must be dealt with or the likelihood of them causing other problems is inevitable. As earlier stated, roots of bitterness spring up, cause trouble and many are defiled because of them. One of the most painful journeys that we can go on is self-examination. It is much easier to take notice of everyone else's shortcomings while refusing to deal with our own. We seem to have a magnifying glass on other people's lives while we refuse to deal with what is in our own hearts. All of us have gifts, but a lot of us have nasty mouths and hearts. So, what, if you have been called to five-fold ministry if you don't have the love of God for your brothers and sisters? Who cares if you are an evangelist if your attitude stinks? Who cares if you are a prophet who can see what is going on with everyone else while idols are filling the crevices of your own heart? It is time to check your heart.

The Elder Brother

While reading the parable of the prodigal son, we typically hear about how the prodigal went away and misused his inheritance, but eventually "came to himself." I have read that story multiple times. What stood out to me this time was the elder brother and his response to both his brother and his father. One would think that the elder brother would have been excited that his younger brother had returned home. However, his reaction to finding out that his brother had returned to a feast, a new robe and ring were quite revealing of a heart issue. While the prodigal son was living a wild, loose life and squandering all his inheritance without a care in the world, his elder brother remained home and took care of the family and farm.

GOD IS....

According to Deuteronomy 21:17, Jewish law allotted for two-thirds of the estate of the deceased to be left to the oldest male child and that son was to take care of the family.

I can imagine that the father knew his youngest son would take the inheritance and throw it away. However, I am sure that he never stopped praying for him and listening for any word of how he was doing from people who would be passing through the area. He probably thought that it was possible that he would never see him again, although he remained hopeful. Every morning, I can see him looking down the same dusty path which he saw his youngest son traveling as he departed, in hopes of seeing him return. One day while the son was on his way back to ask for forgiveness, his father saw him coming back home. The joy he must have felt when he was able to lay his eyes on his child and put his arms around his neck. I have no doubt that the son had probably sold everything that he could in order to survive. His clothes were probably torn; he was probably wearing no shoes and I am sure that he was quite dusty from his long walk home. But I noticed that the father did not condemn him; he did not ask where he had been; he did not discuss his appearance; he did not yell at him for wasting his inheritance but embraced him and put the best robe on him.

The prodigal's father responded much like our heavenly Father after we refuse to accept counsel or instruction. He allows us to go our own way. Even though He knows what is best for us, He will not force us to make decisions or live a life that would be pleasing. God desires our love, but He will not force Himself. He wants us to willingly come to Him. No matter what kinds of bad decisions that we have made, He consistently waits on us to return to Him and when we do, He does not condemn us, but He welcomes us into His forgiveness. He is a loving, kind and forgiving Father.

On the other hand, while the prodigal son had asked for and received forgiveness from his father, his elder brother continued to go about his duties until he heard the laughter and celebration that was taking place. Even though his brother had returned from a lifestyle that had left him broken, he did not share the same attitude that his father did. The elder son had remained in the house the entire time with his father, but the spirit of the father was not in him. While his father was full of compassion and ready to forgive his son, the elder brother was angry, bitter, unforgiving and jealous.

So, it is quite possible to be in the "church", but the love of the

Father does not reside in you. That is a tragic testament to many. How can we attend a church for so long and we still are filled with unforgiveness, strife, bitterness and the like? Scripture plainly tells us that we must forgive those who have wronged us. However, we continually look for reasons not to release those who have offended us. How is it that we can dance, shout and sing all over heart issues and still think that God is pleased with us because we wear our dresses down to our ankles, crosses on our necks and tote our bibles around while the God of the Bible is not in our heart? External appearance is no substitution for internal righteousness. The prodigal looked a mess on the exterior upon his return, yet he had a repentant heart. Repentant sinners will get God's attention long before self-righteous people ever will.

Take time to meditate on these scriptures and allow them to check your heart when Holy Spirit brings correction to you.

Let everyone be quick to hear; slow to speak and slow to wrath; the anger of man does not produce the righteousness of God **(James 1:19-20).**

Do not be eager in your heart to be angry, For anger (rests) dwells in the heart of fools **(Ecclesiastes 7:9 - AMP).**

He who is slow to anger is better and more honorable than the mighty [soldier], And he who rules and controls his own spirit, than he who captures a city **(Proverbs 16:32 - AMP).**

<u>**Hebrews 12:15 (KJV)**</u>	<u>**Hebrews 12:15-17 (Message)**</u>
15 Looking diligently lest any man fail of the grace of God; lest any root of bitterness springing up trouble you, and thereby many be defiled;	14-17 Work at getting along with each other and with God. Otherwise you'll never get so much as a glimpse of God. Make sure no one gets left out of God's generosity. Keep a sharp eye out for weeds of bitter discontent. A thistle or two gone to seed can ruin a whole garden in no time. Watch out for the Esau syndrome: trading away God's lifelong gift in order to satisfy a short-term appetite. You well know how Esau later regretted that impulsive act and wanted God's blessing—but by then it was too late, tears or no tears.
<u>**Proverbs 14:10 (KJV)**</u>	<u>**Proverbs 14:10 (Message)**</u>
10 The heart knoweth his own bitterness, and a stranger doth not intermeddle with his joy.	10 The person who shuns the bitter moments of friends will be an outsider at their celebrations.
<u>**Colossians 3:13 (KJV)**</u>	<u>**Colossians 3:13-14(Message)**</u>
13 Forbearing one another, and forgiving one another, if any man have a quarrel against any: even as Christ forgave you, so also do ye.	12-14 So, chosen by God for this new life of love, dress in the wardrobe God picked out for you: compassion, kindness, humility, quiet strength, discipline. Be even-tempered, content with second place, quick to forgive an offense. Forgive as quickly and completely as the Master forgave you. And regardless of what else

GOD IS....

Psalm 34:18 (KJV)	**Psalm 34:18 (Message)**
¹⁸ The Lord is nigh unto them that are of a broken heart; and saveth such as be of a contrite spirit.	you put on, wear love. It's your basic, all-purpose garment. Never be without it. 18 If your heart is broken, you'll find God right there; if you're kicked in the gut, he'll help you catch your breath.

3

CHAPTER THREE

It's Time for a Heart Check

Unforgiveness causes you to be weighed down and spend far too much time rehearsing what someone else did to wrong you instead of seeking the face of God. Don't forget the beam in your own eye. We have opportunities to be offended on a daily basis, this is why you must guard your heart and not allow an offense to take root. The enemy has no new tricks, so the moment you purpose to walk in forgiveness *intentionally*, you will be tested.

The people who we love the most have the capacity and likelihood to be the very same people who hurt and wound us the most. It is inevitable. I am convinced that God allows us to go through certain seasons in our lives so that we can come to a place of "reckoning."

Through some of my hardest challenges and heartbreak is when Holy Spirit began to severely correct and chastise me. For too long I had placed others in positions that they had no place being. When they disappointed me, did not show the care that I desired or felt I deserved or when I was left feeling abandoned and rejected and spent my time being depressed and oppressed, he showed me that I NEVER should give anyone that kind of power over my joy or peace. He reminded me that before I was formed in my mother's womb me that He had called me and set me apart. He reminded me that He is a jealous God and He would not accept being second to what He had created. There were idols in my heart. Anything or anyone that you revere more than God is an idol and He will have no other gods before Him (Exodus 20:3). So, surgery was needed to remove everything that was not supposed to be there.

I willingly had to get on the operating table so that the master surgeon could do what only He could. There was no anesthesia because He allowed me to revisit each incident of betrayal, pain, sadness, bitterness, rage, loneliness, and rejection. I had to feel it all. All the places that I had attempted to hide away and deceive myself into thinking all those areas really didn't matter had to be brought to the forefront so I could look them square in the eye and identify each one. My enemy was not my loved ones. I had misplaced my frustration and agony of my soul onto others who were just as broken as I was. The only difference was I was the one who confessed how much I loved God and yet my responses to them were anything but how a loving God would respond. How would they ever see the love of the Father when I was not representing Him properly? Yes; I was consistently falsely accused. Yes; my character was assassinated, and I responded out of a wounded, broken heart. No matter how wrong someone else may be; I am still accountable to my creator; my God. I felt like these seasons of crushing and agony were so unfair. Beware of comparing yourself to how others respond in any situation. Your only measuring tool is the Word of God. So, if you are not measuring up by the standard that He has set, it is time for you to deal with those places. Your goal always should be to look like the Father… always.

Oftentimes instead of dealing with the issue, we bury the pain because we have been taught that time heals all things when that is one of the biggest lies ever told. Time alone does not heal our wounds. Many of us are waiting for apologies that may never come and the fact that you forgive or not can't be based on if they ask for it or not (Matthew 6:14-15). No matter what occurs in our lives and who did what to us or what we did, we have a Father who loves and commands that we do the same. WE ARE responsible for our responses. I don't have control over someone else, but I do have control over me.

When He began to remind me of Jesus' complete innocence and the fact that He still carried all sin so that I would not have to; the scales began to fall from my eyes. As I cried out, "God, what have I done to be subjected to this pain?" He reminded me that I prayed daily that He would create in me a clean heart and renew in me a right spirit. In other words, I was getting exactly what I asked for. For the revelation of what had been hiding in the crevices of my heart to manifest, I had to be crushed and it does not feel good. Unbeknownst to me, while asking God to get the glory out of my life, I was also saying, "God, crush me." Now, I have come to a place where I can say, "It was good that I was afflicted" (Psalm 119:71). You might say, "What good thing could possibly come from being crushed." There are many different flowers that must go through this process in order to provide the perfumes that we like. Grapes must be crushed for wine and the olive must undergo extreme pressure in order to produce oil. Then, there is you; you must be crushed so that the anointing can flow from your life.

God is very intentional about your journey. Although you may feel as if you are on this dusty road all alone. Never forget His promise that He will never leave or forsake you. When He feels the light years away is often when He is the closest. Cry out to Him and He will answer. He may not respond like you want Him to; but know whatever His response, it is to further develop and equip you for what lies ahead.

No one likes pain, especially when there seems to be no motive for it. But just like I spent sixteen hours in labor with my first son Reuben eagerly anticipating his arrival. I endured three trimesters of pregnancy, each yielded its own set of challenges and discomfort. It was a difficult natural birth because the "promise" that I was carrying had broad shoulders and weighed 9 pounds, 13 ounces. Many of you are carrying heavy anointings. You have been wondering about all the warfare, sleepless nights, confusion, distractions, and agony of soul. All of this is because of what you are carrying. The price that must be paid is costly but well worth the price. It is not so you can boast in yourself. It is all for the glory of God. Although my second son weighed 10 pounds, 3 ounces his birth was much easier. The process was still the same. I still had to carry him until it was the appointed time. I could not deliver early and expect to have a healthy child. At one point, he had moved in such a way that he was lying on a nerve in my back, which made it difficult to walk because of the shooting pain I felt every time I put my foot on the floor. In fact, I was so physically tired toward the last few weeks of my pregnancy with Austin that I began to complain to my grandmother, and she told me what she did when she was pregnant with one of her children when they were overdue. Her doctor told her to drink Castor Oil which caused her contractions to start and she went into labor. So, what did the good little granddaughter who was tired of what she was carrying do? That's right; I went to the store, got me some Castor Oil and drank the entire bottle. Later that evening I began to have contractions and was excited to go to the hospital because I was determined that I was delivering that baby. Guess what happened next? The doctor came in and determined that I was in labor, however since I was two weeks from my due date, he gave me some medication to stop the contractions and sent me on my way which devastated me. The concern was that the baby needed that additional time in the womb to give all his organs an opportunity to be fully developed. When I finally did deliver him and they saw how big he was, the doctor commented, "If I had known that he was so big, I would have allowed you to deliver."

Don't rush this process. You may be complaining about this and that and asking God how much longer this season will last before the manifestation of what He promised comes forth. Stay the course through all the correction, chastisement, pain and discomfort. Know that in due season and at the appointed time, the promise will manifest.

Questions

1. Do you have people in your life that you refuse to forgive because of something they did to you or something you thought they did?
2. Do you feel like you are justified in not forgiving them?
3. Do you feel as if forgiveness is impossible?

Use the next few pages to write a letter to the people you feel have wronged you even if they are deceased. The pain you may feel is real, but we are commanded to love. Ask the Father to help you release those people. Just as you pray that God forgives you, you must also forgive others.

GOD IS....

Dear _____

_____

_____

_____

_____

_____

_____

_____

_____

_____

_____

_____

_____

_____

_____

_____

_____

_____

_____

_____

_____

> **Psalm 51:10 KJV**
> *Create in me a clean heart, O God; and renew a right spirit within me.*

_____

_____

_____

_____

_____

> **_Jeremiah 17:9-10 (Message)_**
> 9-10 "The heart is hopelessly dark and deceitful, a puzzle that no one can figure out. But I, God, search the heart and examine the mind. I get to the heart of the human. I get to the root of things. I treat them as they really are, not as they pretend to be."

GOD IS....

Proverbs 4:23 (KJV)	**Proverbs 4:23-27 (Message)**
23 Keep thy heart with all diligence; for out of it are the issues of life.	23-27 Keep vigilant watch over your heart; that's where life starts. Don't talk out of both sides of your mouth; avoid careless banter, white lies, and gossip. Keep your eyes straight ahead; ignore all sideshow distractions. Watch your step, and the road will stretch out smooth before you. Look neither right nor left; leave evil in the dust.
Jeremiah 17:9-10 (KJV)	**Jeremiah 17:9-10 (Message)**
9 The heart is deceitful above all things, and desperately wicked: who can know it? 10 I the Lord search the heart, I try the reins, even to give every man according to his ways, and according to the fruit of his doings.	9-10 The heart is hopelessly dark and deceitful, a puzzle that no one can figure out. But I, God, search the heart and examine the mind. I get to the heart of the human. I get to the root of things. I treat them as they really are, not as they pretend to be.
Matthew 15:18-20 (KJV)	**Matthew 15:18-20 (Message)**
18 But those things which proceed out of the mouth come forth from the heart, and they defile the man. 19 For out of the heart proceed evil thoughts, murders, adulteries, fornications, thefts, false witness, blasphemies: 20 These are the things which defile a man: but to eat with unwashed hands defileth not a man.	16-20 Jesus replied, You, too? Are you being willfully stupid? Don't you know that anything that is swallowed works its way through the intestines and is finally defecated? But what comes out of the mouth gets its start in the heart. It's from the heart that we vomit up evil arguments, murders, adulteries, fornications, thefts, lies, and cussing. That's what pollutes. Eating or not eating certain foods, washing or not washing your hands—that's neither here nor there.

CHAPTER FOUR

GOD IS... A Restorer

God is in the business of restoration. Even though the enemy comes to kill, steal and destroy, Jesus came that we would have an abundant life. Have you ever noticed old homes who have been left uncared for throughout the years? The paint is chipped; wooden boards may be loose, rotting or missing and shutters are broken. HGTV is one of my favorite stations and occasionally my mother and I binge watch. I absolutely love to see the houses that were in the worst possible condition and try to imagine what could be done to bring them back to their original design. The architect is the one who is responsible for the design of a building. Therefore, they know exactly, what it should look like as well as how it is designed to function. So, when the contractor attempts to build something that is not on the plans or use materials that have not been approved, the architect has the right and the duty to stop the work until the design is being fully executed.

You may have suffered damage from words that were spoken to you or suffered the consequences of your poor decisions, but God's mind toward you has not changed. His desire is that you would be whole, complete and lacking nothing. In cases where there has been much neglect, sometimes the structure must be completely torn down and rebuilt on the proper foundation.

Before I began working in the construction industry. I had no idea that you could not place a building wherever you decided to put it. A soil analysis must be done in order to make sure that soil is able to hold the foundation. Different parts of the country have different types of soil contents. Some soil is composed of more sand than others which means the unsuitable soil must be removed and new soil trucked in and compacted. Afterward, a geotechnical engineer must test the soil to see if the guidelines have been met. All of this must take place before the foundation can be laid. There would be no use in building a multi-million-dollar structure on a faulty foundation because inevitably when the winds blow hard and the rains come, the building will collapse because the foundation is not equipped to handle the weight. That would be a waste of resources and time.

God is our architect. When He designed us, he had a plan and purpose for all of our lives. Yet for a variety of reasons, some of us have chosen to believe that we are the master of our own fate and we can do as we please without suffering the consequences of decisions that are in direct contradiction to the will of the Father. What we must understand is that God's desire is that we live a life that will mirror who He is. So, if you are looking for what He can give you and not desire Him, you are out of order. The good news is although we have begun to build on faulty soil and foundations. He is ready to show us where we have failed and guide us to reconstruct our lives in such a way that no matter what winds may blow that we are sure that our foundation will never fail. Anything that is to be built spiritually must be built on prayer.

The time that you spend with your Father should never be taken for granted; it is during those quiet times of fellowship that you get to know the heart of the Father. The Holy Spirit is always willing to lead and guide us into all truth. We tend to spend too much time running to tell Him what we want and never seem to ask what He desires. Have you ever thought about sitting in the presence of God without a list and see what He wants to say? Find you a quiet place and just sit. Ask God to show you where you have not been attentive to what needs correcting in your life. We typically find it so much easier to see what is wrong with everyone else, but we cannot hear what He is saying that needs restoring or correcting in our lives. Whatever you may need for God to restore He is more than able to do far beyond everything that we think or ask of Him and there is nothing that is too hard for Him. You may feel as though there is no help for you because you have been a particular way for as long as you can remember. However, there is help and hope for you so stop hiding and get healed for real. You must be desperate for Him. If you have no expectation, then you will get what you expect, which is nothing. Our God is a restorer of relationships and bodies. He can take that which was broken and lifeless and breathe new life into it. Instead of "focusing externally" turn your attention inward. For when we begin to take a hard look at who we really are and stop believing the lie that "we are good," we will begin to freely give to others the grace that we ourselves desire. How is it that we say we love God and do not love God's creation?

5

CHAPTER FIVE

GOD IS… Your Defense

As with any altercation, whether it is physical or spiritual our tendency is to protect ourselves and not allow our opponent to get the best of us. The awareness of your adversary and his tactics are very important. Since we know the enemy has no new tricks, we must use wisdom in dealing with his lies. Revelation 12 tells us about the accuser of our brethren who accuses us before God day and night. He is a cunning deceiver who wants to destroy you. One of the first things he comes after is your mind. He wants you to believe that you cannot be forgiven for the things that you have done in the past or cause you to become so full of guilt and shame that you are paralyzed from pursuing the Father because you believe the lie that God could have no use of you. I need you to understand that the Bible is full of people who had problems in their flesh; rebellion, pride, anger issues, infidelities, idol worship, unfaithfulness and yet those were the people that God chose to carry out His will. God seems to take great pleasure in turning the ugliest situations into beautiful songs. What you may have thought were the things that could or would disqualify you are the same things that God can use to set others free. The trials, tests, and heartbreak that you have endured are not for you only. Frankly, your warfare is not personal. Sometimes, we think that no one else has gone through what we have, and that is not true. Shame, guilt, and condemnation have kept us from sharing our testimonies of how God set us free and delivered us. Many are still bound in the prison of their own minds because they fear what others may say. Satan targets our minds and he loves to replay our sin before us saying such things as, "What would people say if they knew what you did? Everyone is laughing at you. How can you ever amount to anything when your own daddy did not want you? You keep doing the same things repeatedly; God will never keep forgiving you. There is no use in trying to serve God; He hasn't answered your prayers, so why serve Him?"

GOD IS....

The Book of Job describes him as a prosperous, wealthy man who was blessed with cattle, servants, and children. When the sons of God presented themselves before the Lord, the enemy (Satan) came too. God apparently asked Satan had he considered his servant Job because there was none like him in the earth. God referred to Job as a perfect and upright man (Job 1).

This conversation leads me to believe that the enemy very well could have had a conversation with God concerning you. The enemy told God that the only reason that Job served Him was that there was a hedge around him and everything that he owned. So, when Job's children died and he lost his property, even his friends assumed that he must have done something wrong. Have you ever thought that sometimes the reason that you have gone through some very tough circumstances and situations and even your friends turned their back on you was because you were chosen so that others may see what it looks like to have your back against the wall; lose family, friends, jobs, houses and cars only to still keep blessing God when others would have cursed Him? That is something to ponder. There is nothing like being falsely accused. Someone who was dear to me made some very serious accusations. They were unfounded on every level. I could not begin to digest how much it hurt and wounded me. There was no way that the accusations were remotely possible or true. I was completely innocent and yet heartbroken. I immediately recognized that my adversary was at work. Even though I was hurt, I quickly understood that what the enemy wanted me to do was to attempt to defend myself against a lie and be offended. Furthermore, he wanted me to hold a grudge and be bitter. Prior to this event, I could feel something brewing; I just could not put my finger on it. There was an uneasy "feeling" that I had and knew something just was not right. A couple of weeks prior, I had given God a fresh "Yes." Instead of continuing to hide from the totality of what I knew, God was requiring of me because I was afraid, I made up my mind that I would not live the last years of my life in fear. I refused to be afraid of failure; afraid of the opinions of others and afraid that I would be rejected again. There were times I would recall the Bible story regarding Abram when the Lord told him to leave his country, the people that he was familiar with and his household and go to a land that He would show him (Genesis 12).

I only knew a part of what God's directions and instructions were. I did not have the road map that I felt that I needed and desired to complete the task. At times, I would be paralyzed by what I was seeing and hearing. Like Abram, who disobediently brought Lot with him, I tried to grab people along with me when God had not ordained it to be so. I came to understand that I could not share my dreams with certain people. So, I paid the consequences of my disobedience.

People will look at you like you are crazy when you begin to share. At the time, I did not understand why I felt the loneliness. I am an only child and I am quite accustomed to being alone. The truth is, I enjoy my own company. Those times are when I can listen intently to the Father's voice and ask questions about the things that have hindered my walk with Him or that have not been pleasing. I thought I had gotten through some of these areas. That is one of the things that I love about God when you are open to His correction, He will show you things about yourself that you thought you had dealt with.

In 2003, I wrote one of my first books titled *Rejection: Triumph over Disappointments*. Part of my healing came by writing some intimate details of my life. As the years went by, I began to understand that deliverance can take place in stages; much like the onion, the layers of my life are continually being pulled back. Therefore, when the enemy began to use people to falsely accuse me initially, I was crushed. Although the enemy had constructed and issued a severe blow to me this time, I was surprised at my immediate response. Part of my daily prayers include asking God to create in me a clean heart. I knew that in the years prior that I was angry and bitter over being wronged, misunderstood and rejected. There was a lot of work that needed to be done and the Holy Spirit needed to do was not easy. Instead of focusing on the perpetrators, I had to turn my focus on myself and be more concerned with my responses.

One morning while I was praying and meditating the Holy Spirit began to talk to me about what it would be like if I needed surgery and how important it is that the doctor who performs the procedure have properly sterilized surgical instruments. Pain is an indicator that something is wrong and once the pain is more than a Tylenol will take care of, we typically will find our way to the doctor who will then assess and diagnose our symptoms. Based on what the doctor finds while we are being examined, it could be determined that a surgical procedure is necessary. If you have ever had surgery, you understand that the room and everything that is in the room must be sterile in order to ensure that there is limited opportunity for infection. Even though your doctor may be a skilled physician, they rely on surgical utensils to help them to do an operation. Now, if those surgical tools have not been sterilized properly then once used on a patient, there is an increased likelihood of infection taking place.

So, consider yourself for a moment. You may be an intercessor, operating in a fivefold grace (pastor, apostle, prophet, evangelist, teacher) and may stand before others to teach, prophesy, lay hands, cast out devils and the like; but if your vessel is not clean, you are doing nothing more than infecting the very people you are supposed to help. If you are not healed and delivered the very people that God has called, you to help heal can suffer further damage and even spiritual death because you refuse to deal with your stuff. Every single one of us has had to deal with many obstacles and yet our hearts must remain pure and undefiled. You will be consistently challenged and opposed. Your adversary wants to cause you to be ineffective in your assignment and ultimately cause you to be impotent and unfruitful.

Even though my heart felt as if it were broken into a million pieces, I knew this time that my "yes" was different from other times.

I had gained strength through prayer, praise, and extensive fasting. My flesh had to be crushed and if you want to know what truly lies in the crevices of your soul abstain from food for extended periods of time and you will find our more than you want to know. Fasting should not be something you do once a year. It should be a lifestyle.

For me, whenever there was an assignment, fresh revelation or a prophetic word the pattern was that the enemy was going to show his ugly head to distract, discourage and detour me from what I needed to be focused on. Too many times I had allowed these distractions to pull me away and depression and self-pity would set in and cause me to rehearse past failures, mistakes, and trauma. This time I made up my mind that I would not fall prey to the same tricks. My focus would not be shifted, and I refused to stop pursuing God and fulfil the purpose I was sent into the earth to complete. There is a reason and purpose why we all are here. God is trying to perfect us, and He is intentional. Even the things that God has allowed into your life have a purpose. Your poor choices may have caused you some trouble, but God can even take your missteps and mess ups and get glory out of it. People cannot give you what they do not have to give. Release people from your unrealistic expectations. They are not God;

God is.

Be Thankful

During the many seasons of our lives, we must always be thankful. While life happens to all of us, how we respond is vitally important. God knows about every up and down that we are going to undertake and no matter what may befall us, He is still faithful. Whether we are believing for loved ones to be saved; trusting God for healing in our mind and body or waiting for the manifestation of promises, our God is faithful through it all. Even as Job was confident that no matter what state he was in or no matter what he had lost, he was not going to curse God. Whatever you stand in need of is in the hands of God. He is our provider and while I sometimes wish that I could hide and not face some very unpleasant circumstance, I know that it is all a part of my process. The crushing that takes place will produce oil, but it will also produce pain.

Heaven's announcements can come by prophetic words given through individuals, the Word of God, or by dreams and visions. These announcements, as I like to call them, could be to warn, encourage or give you insight into coming events regarding your future. Our adversary and his cohorts are neither omniscient nor omnipresent. He does not know everything and cannot be everywhere at once. Satan does not know specifics. He has been around a long time so he can sense when God is about to do something. He may notice angelic activity around a soul, etc. So, it may seem that as soon as you receive a prophetic word from the man or woman of God, that all hell seems to break loose. Think about this for a moment. The word for your life has now been released in the atmosphere and while the enemy beforehand may not have had specifics regarding what God has planned, now he and his minions have heard the word and know how to wage warfare against you and what God has designed to manifest in your life. That is why it seems that immediately after you get this awesome word of prophecy that you seem to go into spiritual warfare.

At the end of this book, there is a section for you to document what God is saying about you, your family and your ministry. Don't rely on your memory. You must write them down so you will be able to revisit them later and decree the Word of the Lord. It is important to recognize that the enemy likes to talk too. God will never tell you anything that is contrary to His Word. Therefore, if it does not line up, then you know that it was not the Word of the Lord.

The Woes (Distress, Great Sorrow) of David- The Warrior

As we look at the life of David, we often think if his victories. How he slew the bear and the lion and the many military conquests that he encountered. We may not think as much about his "process." David had to go through much adversity in order to receive the promises and walk out his God-ordained purpose in the earth. The Lord tells Samuel to go to Jesse's house and anoint the next King. I am sure that the other brothers were surprised at the fact that David, who initially was not even among them when the prophet came to the house, was anointed to be the next King of Israel. David did not look like what everyone assumed a king should look.

I can tell you right now that people may be looking at you because they cannot understand how or why God would or could use you or me. They may know your mama and daddy and everyone else in your family and would not believe that God has ordained you to be the next apostle, prophet, pastor, evangelist, teacher, CEO, bank executive, entrepreneur, college professor or anything else for that matter. According to others your life may have started out and gone from bad to worse, but that still does not mean that you were not destined for greatness. Remember, that God knows the thoughts that he has concerning you, and they are to give you a future and a hope. Stay focused on the plan that He has for your life and do not waiver. Man will look on your outward appearance and size up where they think your future is and treat you according to what they "think" you will have or what you can obtain. David's own father did not think enough of his son to include him in the initial invitation and bring him before the prophet like his other sons. He was the youngest of his siblings and deemed the "least likely to succeed" by members of his family. Let this be a lesson to you that when it is your season to be promoted and brought to the forefront, it will not matter where you are geographically located. God knows how to locate you. You don't need to jockey for position and cozy up to who you may think can introduce you to the right people when it is the proper time. Promotion comes from God and He knows exactly where to find you when it is time for you to be elevated.

You may think that you are too young naturally or spiritually. Do not despise small beginnings or allow the fact that no one seems to know your name or where you have come from. God chooses who He desires to use and has a specific purpose in mind for you. Do not allow your struggles to make you think that God has forgotten about you. You are constantly on the mind of God. You are being perfected, challenged, stretched and even chastised, purged and cleansed for your next assignment. Do not grow faint or lose heart because of the road you are currently traveling. God's Word cannot lie. What you must understand is that there is something that you must learn in every stage of your journey. When you are in an obscure place, know that this is your season of preparation. Too many people want to be anointed but do not want to be processed for their purpose.

I want to remind you that even though the Word of God has made certain declarations regarding who you are and that before God formed you in the womb that He knew you (Jeremiah 1:5), you cannot think that there won't be trials, setbacks, calamities and misunderstandings along the way. All these things are a part of the process that has been ordained for your life.

When Samuel determined that the sons that Jesse brought before him were not who God had chosen, Samuel inquired if there was another son. Imagine how everyone, including David, initially felt as he brought himself before the prophet of God unkempt and smelling like sheep. He must have been embarrassed at his appearance. I am sure that the other sons had groomed themselves in preparation to receive the prophet into their home. Let that simply be a reminder to you that outward appearance does not matter. God is looking at the state of your heart.

David was anointed on three separate occasions. After his initial meeting with Samuel, he began to serve Saul, who was also a part of his training. How you handle each stage of this training has a direct impact on your elevation. You may be crying out for elevation, but can you handle the level you are on now? Can you handle the warfare you are enduring now? Have you defeated the spiritual enemies that are currently on your trail? Do you honor those who you are assigned to now although the enemy may be using them the try and take you out? Are you able to recognize that through all of this, God is only shaping your character so that when He does place you where He desires that you are stable and understand that your allegiance is to Him and not a man?

Take a little time and read the scriptures at the end of this chapter to gain greater clarity and understanding regarding David's journey. You may be anointed for a specific service, but it does not mean that you will not meet with opposition. The fact that you are anointed should clue you in that through it all that God remains faithful and in order for you to properly glorify Him; you too must remain faithful. The very last thing that you should want is a premature promotion because it will yield a catastrophic outcome. You should never want anything before the right time.

You would not dare want to eat a cake that has not remained in the oven for the specified time in order to ensure that it is good for consumption. You should never want to move out in the things of God without knowing that the people you have been assigned to serve will not be contaminated because you are not healed and whole.

There were times that David had an opportunity to take vengeance out on Saul. He did not raise his hand to bring harm to the King who had been anointed by God. David understood the place of honor even when Saul was acting dishonorably. No one would have probably faulted David for protecting himself. But David's reliance was in God. He trusted His Father to defend him even when the odds were stacked against him. I am convinced that David would not have been able to write 73 of the Psalms without having gone through those intense moments of betrayal, heartbreak, confusion, and sadness. He was qualified to write them even during those seasons when he made some gut-wrenching errors in judgment. In the middle of it all, he cried out to God and He answered him.

Whatever befell David, God showed that He was trustworthy and dependable over and over again. He has not changed. He is the same yesterday, today and forever. He is still trustworthy and dependable, and He is capable of defending you. Where we have often made mistakes is that we think that we can take care of ourselves. We often create a bigger problem because, at times, it seems that God has forgotten that we have been wronged and feel like we need to vindicate ourselves when He knows far better what we need and when it should manifest. Isn't it funny that we want people to suffer consequences quickly when we ourselves want the wheels of justice to be slow?

David's Journey

* David was anointed by Samuel to be King – I Samuel 16
* David entered the service of Saul
* David kills Goliath – I Samuel 17
* David set over the men of war by Saul – I Samuel 18
* Saul attempts to kill David with the spear
* Saul places David over a thousand – I Samuel 18:13

GOD IS....

* David marries Michal
* Saul tried to kill David
* David hides in the cave of Adullum – I Samuel 22
* David spares Saul's life on two separate occasions – I Samuel 24, 26
* Amalekites take the wives of David's men – I Samuel 28
* David assumes control of Judah and is anointed King – 2 Samuel 2:7
* David anointed King over all Israel – 2 Samuel 5:17

It is interesting to note that although David had great victories, he also encountered great suffering, trials, and tests. Be encouraged that no matter how many setbacks you may have, your obedience to God through it all will position you for victory and promotions.

6

CHAPTER SIX

GOD IS...Love

I pray that as you have journeyed through this book that you have learned that whatever you have gone through in life; good or bad, that it was not meant to kill you but to propel you. Who would have thought that you would be where you are right now? You have made it through some horrendous circumstances and yet God still brought you through them all. The compassionate love of your Heavenly Father has been leading and guiding you every step of the way. He loved us enough to carry our guilt, shame, fear, disobedience hatred, perversion, and every other sin in order that we would be free.

GOD IS....

I want to talk to you about how much God loves you. You may be thinking the complete opposite, because how could a loving Father allow you to endure such trials and not come to your immediate rescue? That just would not seem to make natural sense. How could His pain equal our freedom? I have a question for you? What pain are you willing to carry in order to see people free? I know that you are thinking that only the blood of Jesus could pay the price for sin, which is true. However, you can help others overcome with your testimony. "And they overcame him by the blood of the Lamb, and by the word of their testimony; and they loved not their lives unto the death" (Rev.12:11). Be transparent enough to wisely share your testimony with others who could benefit and may have suffered similar circumstances. They need to know that God will see them through as well. The muzzle that the enemy has placed over your mouth because of the shame and embarrassment of your past must be removed. Remember, you did not travel this rocky road to leave your brothers and sisters wandering in the dark while you now have a road map about how to get out of the valley. Help them; encourage them and let them know that they have the victory.

Often, we look at all the bad things that have happened in our lives as a terrible set of circumstances. Let me remind you that God is intentional about every aspect of our existence. He can even take our bad choices and use them for our good if we allow Him to turn them into teaching moments. You may have questions such as, "Why was I raped; why wasn't I loved; why didn't my parents care for me properly or why was I abused?" I do not have the answers but I do know that your life has value and you have a purpose (something set up as an object or end to be attained) and a destiny (a predetermined course of events often held to be an irresistible power or agency – Merriam-Webster). You may think that your life does not look like much right now, but I encourage you to embrace the Word of God as your blueprint and roadmap so you can get to your final destination. There will be hills and valleys but remember that the steps of a good (righteous) man are ordered. It may not make any sense to you at all why you must travel this road. This is why it is absolutely necessary for you to develop your own personal relationship with the Father. His voice is who you should yield your ears to continually so you will have no problem recognizing who you are listening to and obeying whatever He says. Whenever you become truly familiar with the Father's voice that you can easily obey Him in the 'hard' areas because you know that He will never lead you the wrong way. It is His love that will sustain you in the darkest times of your life. He is a faithful Father and He can be trusted.

God placed our guilt upon Jesus to bear for us all, even though He was innocent. He never defended Himself or called for the legions of angels who would have come to His aid because Jesus knew that His Father had the ultimate plan for civilization; to once and for all be made sin so that we could enjoy the benefits of being Kingdom citizens. Our faith and trust in God are what will keep us in proper alignment with His will for us. There was a recent season in my life when I thought I just could not take the pressure anymore and after crying myself to sleep, I had a dream that I looked up and all I saw was two big, white, pulsating words….. TRUST ME and over the course of the night, every time I turned over those same two words were glaring at me….. TRUST ME. If you don't remember anything else that has been written in this book, understand that your God loves you and He can be trusted. He promised that He will never leave or forsake you and even when you cannot feel Him; He is near. "The Lord is close to the brokenhearted and saves those who are crushed in spirit" (Psalm 34:18 NIV).

Read the scripture below and remember what the precious shed blood of Jesus did for you. He was bruised and wounded so that you can be healed and whole from the inside out. Simply put; GOD IS..

Isaiah 53 (The Message Bible)
1 Who believes what we've heard and seen?
Who would have thought God's saving power would look like this?

2-6 The servant grew up before God—a scrawny seedling,
   a scrubby plant in a parched field.
There was nothing attractive about him,
   nothing to cause us to take a second look.
He was looked down on and passed over,
   a man who suffered, who knew pain firsthand.
One look at him and people turned away.
   We looked down on him, thought he was scum.
But the fact is, it was our pains he carried—
   our disfigurements, all the things wrong with us.
We thought he brought it on himself,
   that God was punishing him for his own failures.
But it was our sins that did that to him,
   that ripped and tore and crushed him—our sins!
He took the punishment, and that made us whole.
   Through his bruises, we get healed.
We're all like sheep who've wandered off and gotten lost.
   We've all done our own thing, gone our own way.
And God has piled all our sins, everything we've done wrong,

on him, on him.

7-9 He was beaten, he was tortured,
   but he didn't say a word.
Like a lamb was taken to be slaughtered
   and like a sheep being sheared,
   he took it all in silence.
Justice miscarried, and he was led off—
   and did anyone really know what was happening?
He died without a thought for his own welfare,
   beaten bloody for the sins of my people.
They buried him with the wicked,
   threw him in a grave with a rich man,
Even though he'd never hurt a soul
   or said one word that wasn't true.

10 Still, it's what God had in mind all along,
   to crush him with pain.
The plan was that he give himself as an offering for sin
   so that he'd see life come from it—life, life, and more life.
   And God's plan will deeply prosper through him.

11-12 Out of that terrible travail of soul,
   he'll see that it's worth it and be glad he did it.
Through what he experienced, my righteous one, my servant,
   will make many "righteous ones,"
   as he himself carries the burden of their sins.
Therefore, I'll reward him extravagantly—

>   the best of everything, the highest honors—
> Because he looked death in the face and didn't flinch,
>   because he embraced the company of the lowest.
> He took on his own shoulders the sin of the many,
>   he took up the cause of all the black sheep.

GOD IS....

Heaven's Prophetic Announcements

Use the following pages to journal the prophetic words that have been released over your life. You will need to document and revisit them often. Remember the enemy does not want you to know who you are or walk in all that God has ordained for you.
Remember… GOD IS…

Timothy, my son, I am giving you this command in keeping with the prophecies once made about you so that by recalling them you may fight the battle well.
I Timothy 1:18

Heaven's Prophetic Announcement

Date_____

Prophetic Word Released By/Through:

_____

_____
_____
_____
_____
_____
_____
_____
_____
_____

When and how did this word manifest?

_____
_____
_____
_____

GOD IS....

Timothy, my son, I am giving you this command in keeping with the prophecies once made about you so that by recalling them you may fight the battle well.
I Timothy 1:18

Heaven's Prophetic Announcement

Date_____

Prophetic Word Released By/Through:

_____

_____
_____
_____
_____
_____
_____
_____
_____
_____
_____

When and how did this word manifest?

_____
_____
_____
_____

Timothy, my son, I am giving you this command in keeping with the prophecies once made about you so that by recalling them you may fight the battle well.
I Timothy 1:18

Heaven's Prophetic Announcement

Date_____

Prophetic Word Released By/Through:

_____

_____
_____
_____
_____
_____
_____
_____
_____
_____

When and how did this word manifest?

_____
_____
_____
_____

GOD IS....

Timothy, my son, I am giving you this command in keeping with the prophecies once made about you so that by recalling them you may fight the battle well.
I Timothy 1:18

Heaven's Prophetic Announcement
Date_____

Prophetic Word Released By/Through:
_____

_____
_____
_____
_____
_____
_____
_____
_____
_____
_____
_____

When and how did this word manifest?
_____
_____
_____

Timothy, my son, I am giving you this command in keeping with the prophecies once made about you so that by recalling them you may fight the battle well.
I Timothy 1:18

Heaven's Prophetic Announcement
Date_____

Prophetic Word Released By/Through:
_____

_____
_____
_____
_____
_____
_____
_____
_____
_____

When and how did this word manifest?
_____
_____
_____
_____
_____

GOD IS....

Timothy, my son, I am giving you this command in keeping with the prophecies once made about you so that by recalling them you may fight the battle well.
I Timothy 1:18

Heaven's Prophetic Announcement

Date_____

Prophetic Word Released By/Through:

_____

_____
_____
_____
_____
_____
_____
_____
_____
_____
_____

When and how did this word manifest?

_____
_____
_____
_____

Timothy, my son, I am giving you this command in keeping with the prophecies once made about you so that by recalling them you may fight the battle well.
I Timothy 1:18

Heaven's Prophetic Announcement

Date_____

Prophetic Word Released By/Through:
_____

_____
_____
_____
_____
_____
_____
_____
_____
_____
_____

When and how did this word manifest?
_____
_____
_____
_____

GOD IS....

Timothy, my son, I am giving you this command in keeping with the prophecies once made about you so that by recalling them you may fight the battle well.
I Timothy 1:18

Heaven's Prophetic Announcement
Date_____

Prophetic Word Released By/Through:
_____

_____
_____
_____
_____
_____
_____
_____
_____
_____
_____

When and how did this word manifest?
_____
_____
_____
_____
_____
_____

Timothy, my son, I am giving you this command in keeping with the prophecies once made about you so that by recalling them you may fight the battle well.
I Timothy 1:18

Heaven's Prophetic Announcement
Date_____

Prophetic Word Released By/Through:
_____

What warfare did you notice began after receiving this word?
_____
_____
_____
_____
_____
_____
_____
_____

When and how did this word manifest?
_____
_____
_____
_____
_____

GOD IS....

Timothy, my son, I am giving you this command in keeping with the prophecies once made about you so that by recalling them you may fight the battle well.
I Timothy 1:18

Heaven's Prophetic Announcement

Date_____

Prophetic Word Released By/Through:

_____

What warfare did you notice began after receiving this word?

_____
_____
_____
_____
_____
_____
_____
_____
_____

When and how did this word manifest?

_____
_____
_____
_____
_____

Timothy, my son, I am giving you this command in keeping with the prophecies once made about you so that by recalling them you may fight the battle well.
I Timothy 1:18

Heaven's Prophetic Announcement

Date_____

Prophetic Word Released By/Through:

_____

What warfare did you notice began after receiving this word?

_____
_____
_____
_____
_____
_____
_____
_____

When and how did this word manifest?

_____
_____
_____
_____
_____

GOD IS....

Timothy, my son, I am giving you this command in keeping with the prophecies once made about you so that by recalling them you may fight the battle well.
I Timothy 1:18

Heaven's Prophetic Announcement
Date_____

Prophetic Word Released By/Through:
_____

What warfare did you notice began after receiving this word?
_____
_____
_____
_____
_____
_____
_____
_____
_____

When and how did this word manifest?
_____
_____
_____
_____
_____

Timothy, my son, I am giving you this command in keeping with the prophecies once made about you so that by recalling them you may fight the battle well.
I Timothy 1:18

Heaven's Prophetic Announcement
Date_____

Prophetic Word Released By/Through:
_____

What warfare did you notice began after receiving this word?
_____
_____
_____
_____
_____
_____
_____
_____

When and how did this word manifest?
_____
_____
_____
_____
_____

GOD IS....

Timothy, my son, I am giving you this command in keeping with the prophecies once made about you so that by recalling them you may fight the battle well.
I Timothy 1:18

Heaven's Prophetic Announcement
Date_____

Prophetic Word Released By/Through:
_____

What warfare did you notice began after receiving this word?
_____
_____
_____
_____
_____
_____
_____
_____
_____

When and how did this word manifest?
_____
_____
_____
_____

Timothy, my son, I am giving you this command in keeping with the prophecies once made about you so that by recalling them you may fight the battle well.
I Timothy 1:18

Heaven's Prophetic Announcement

Date_____

Prophetic Word Released By/Through:

_____

What warfare did you notice began after receiving this word?

_____
_____
_____
_____
_____
_____
_____
_____

When and how did this word manifest?

_____
_____
_____
_____

GOD IS....

Timothy, my son, I am giving you this command in keeping with the prophecies once made about you so that by recalling them you may fight the battle well.
I Timothy 1:18

Heaven's Prophetic Announcement

Date_____

Prophetic Word Released By/Through:
_____

What warfare did you notice began after receiving this word?
_____
_____
_____
_____
_____
_____
_____
_____

When and how did this word manifest?
_____
_____
_____
_____
_____

Timothy, my son, I am giving you this command in keeping with the prophecies once made about you so that by recalling them you may fight the battle well.
I Timothy 1:18

Heaven's Prophetic Announcement
Date_____

Prophetic Word Released By/Through:
_____

What warfare did you notice began after receiving this word?
_____
_____
_____
_____
_____
_____
_____
_____

When and how did this word manifest?
_____
_____
_____
_____
_____

GOD IS....

Timothy, my son, I am giving you this command in keeping with the prophecies once made about you so that by recalling them you may fight the battle well.
I Timothy 1:18

Heaven's Prophetic Announcement
Date_____

Prophetic Word Released By/Through:
_____

What warfare did you notice began after receiving this word?
_____
_____
_____
_____
_____
_____
_____
_____
_____

When and how did this word manifest?
_____
_____
_____
_____
_____

Timothy, my son, I am giving you this command in keeping with the prophecies once made about you so that by recalling them you may fight the battle well.
I Timothy 1:18

Heaven's Prophetic Announcement

Date_____

Prophetic Word Released By/Through:

_____

What warfare did you notice began after receiving this word?

_____
_____
_____
_____
_____
_____
_____
_____

When and how did this word manifest?

_____
_____
_____
_____
_____

GOD IS....

Timothy, my son, I am giving you this command in keeping with the prophecies once made about you so that by recalling them you may fight the battle well.
I Timothy 1:18

Heaven's Prophetic Announcement
Date_____

Prophetic Word Released By/Through:
_____

What warfare did you notice began after receiving this word?
_____
_____
_____
_____
_____
_____
_____
_____
_____

When and how did this word manifest?
_____
_____
_____
_____
_____
_____

GOD IS....

(Numbers 23:19 NIV) **God is** not a man, that he should lie, nor a son of man, that he should change his mind. Does he speak and then not act? Does he promise and not fulfill?

(Deuteronomy 4:24 NIV) For the LORD your **God is** a consuming fire, a jealous God.

(Deuteronomy 4:31 NIV) For the LORD your **God is** a merciful God; he will not abandon or destroy you or forget the covenant with your forefathers, which he confirmed to them by oath.

(Deuteronomy 9:3 NIV) But be assured today that the LORD your **God is** the one who goes across ahead of you like a devouring fire. He will destroy them; he will subdue them before you. And you will drive them out and annihilate them quickly, as the LORD has promised you.

(Deuteronomy 10:17 NIV) For the LORD your **God is** God of gods and Lord of lords, the great God, mighty and awesome, who shows no partiality and accepts no bribes.

(Deuteronomy 20:4 NIV) For the LORD your **God is** the one who goes with you to fight for you against your enemies to give you victory."

(Deuteronomy 33:27 NIV) The eternal **God is** your refuge, and underneath are the everlasting arms. He will drive out your enemy before you, saying, 'Destroy him!'

(Joshua 1:8-9 NIV) Do not let this Book of the Law depart from your mouth; meditate on it day and night, so that you may be careful to do everything written in it. Then you will be prosperous and successful. {9} Have I not commanded you? Be strong and courageous. Do not be terrified; do not be discouraged, for the LORD your God will be with you wherever you go."

(2 Chronicles 30:9 NIV) If you return to the LORD, then your brothers and your children will be shown compassion by their captors and will come back to this land, for the LORD your **God is** gracious and compassionate. He will not turn his face from you if you return to him."

(Ezra 8:22 NIV) I was ashamed to ask the king for soldiers and horsemen to protect us from enemies on the road, because we had told the king, "The gracious hand of our **God is** on everyone who looks to him, but his great anger is against all who forsake him."

(Psalms 33:11-13 NIV) But the plans of the LORD stand firm forever, the purposes of his heart through all generations. {12} Blessed is the nation whose **God is** the LORD, the people he chose for his inheritance. {13} From heaven the LORD looks down and sees all mankind;

(Psalms 37:30-31 NIV) The mouth of the righteous man utters wisdom, and his tongue speaks what is just. {31} The law of his **God is** in his heart; his feet do not slip.

(Psalms 46:1-2 NIV) For the director of music. Of the Sons of Korah. According to alamoth. A song. **God is** our refuge and strength, an ever-present help in trouble. {2} Therefore we will not fear, though the earth give way and the mountains fall into the heart of the sea,

(Psalms 46:4-5 NIV) There is a river whose streams make glad the city of God, the holy place where the Most High dwells. {5} **God is** within her; she will not fall; God will help her at the break of day.

(Psalms 48:14 NIV) For this **God is** our God for ever and ever; he will be our guide even to the end.

(Psalms 54:4 NIV) Surely **God is** my help; the Lord is the one who sustains me.

(Psalms 62:7-8 NIV) My salvation and my honor depend on God; he is my mighty rock, my refuge. {8} Trust in him at all times, O people; pour out your hearts to him, for **God is** our refuge. Selah

(Psalms 68:19-20 NIV) Praise be to the Lord, to God our Savior, who daily bears our burdens. Selah {20} Our **God is** a God who saves; from the Sovereign LORD comes escape from death.

(Psalms 73:26 NIV) My flesh and my heart may fail, but **God is** the strength of my heart and my portion forever.

(Psalms 84:11-12 NIV) For the LORD **God is** a sun and shield; the LORD bestows favor and honor; no good thing does he withhold from those whose walk is blameless. {12} O LORD Almighty, blessed is the man who trusts in you.

(Psalms 116:5 NIV) The LORD is gracious and righteous; our **God is** full of compassion.

(Psalms 144:15 NIV) Blessed are the people of whom this is true; blessed are the people whose **God is** the LORD.

(Proverbs 30:5 NIV) "Every word of **God is** flawless; he is a shield to those who take refuge in him.

(Isaiah 61:1-3 NIV) The Spirit of the Sovereign LORD is on me, because the LORD has anointed me to preach good news to the poor. He has sent me to bind up the brokenhearted, to proclaim freedom for the captives and release from darkness for the prisoners, {2} to proclaim the year of the Lord's favor and the day of vengeance of our God, to comfort all who mourn, {3} and provide for those who grieve in Zion– to bestow on them a crown of beauty instead of ashes, the oil of gladness instead of mourning, and a garment of praise instead of a spirit of despair. They will be called oaks of righteousness, a planting of the LORD for the display of his splendor.

GOD IS....

(Mark 1:15 NIV) "The time has come," he said. "The kingdom of **God is** near. Repent and believe the good news!"

(Luke 7:28 NIV) I tell you, among those born of women there is no one greater than John; yet the one who is least in the kingdom of **God is** greater than he."

(Luke 10:9 NIV) Heal the sick who are there and tell them, 'The kingdom of **God is** near you.'

(Luke 16:16 NIV) "The Law and the Prophets were proclaimed until John. Since that time, the good news of the kingdom of **God is** being preached, and everyone is forcing his way into it.

(Luke 17:21 NIV) nor will people say, 'Here it is,' or 'There it is,' because the kingdom of **God is** within you."

(John 4:24 NIV) **God is** spirit, and his worshipers must worship in spirit and in truth."

(John 6:33 NIV) For the bread of **God is** he who comes down from heaven and gives life to the world."

(Romans 6:23 NIV) For the wages of sin is death, but the gift of **God is** eternal life in Christ Jesus our Lord.

(Romans 14:17 NIV) For the kingdom of **God is** not a matter of eating and drinking, but of righteousness, peace and joy in the Holy Spirit,

(1 Corinthians 4:20 NIV) For the kingdom of **God is** not a matter of talk but of power.

(1 Corinthians 10:13 NIV) No temptation has seized you except what is common to man. And **God is** faithful; he will not let you be tempted beyond what you can bear. But when you are tempted, he will also provide a way out so that you can stand up under it.

(1 Corinthians 14:33 NIV) For **God is** not a God of disorder but of peace. As in all the congregations of the saints,

(2 Corinthians 9:8 NIV) And **God is** able to make all grace abound to you, so that in all things at all times, having all that you need, you will abound in every good work.

GOD IS....

(Hebrews 4:12 NIV) For the word of **God is** living and active. Sharper than any double-edged sword, it penetrates even to dividing soul and spirit, joints and marrow; it judges the thoughts and attitudes of the heart.

(Hebrews 11:16 NIV) Instead, they were longing for a better country—a heavenly one. Therefore, **God is** not ashamed to be called their God, for he has prepared a city for them.

(Hebrews 13:16 NIV) And do not forget to do good and to share with others, for with such sacrifices **God is** pleased.

(1 John 1:5 NIV) This is the message we have heard from him and declare to you: **God is** light; in him there is no darkness at all.

(1 John 4:7-9 NIV) Dear friends, let us love one another, for love comes from God. Everyone who loves has been born of God and knows God. {8} Whoever does not love does not know God, because **God is** love. {9} This is how God showed his love among us: He sent his one and only Son into the world that we might live through him.

(1 John 4:16 NIV) And so we know and rely on the love God has for us. **God is** love. Whoever lives in love lives in God, and God in him.

(Revelation 21:3 NIV) And I heard a loud voice from the throne saying, "Now the dwelling of **God is** with men, and he will live with them. They will be his people, and God himself will be with them and be their God.

About the Author

Enger Lanier Taylor is a native of Huntsville, Alabama. She earned her B.S. degree in Business Administration with a concentration in Logistics and Procurement from Alabama A&M University in 1989. For the past 28 years, she has been employed by the City of Huntsville. She is also a licensed real estate agent, an award-winning author and a faithful member of Abounding

Love Ministries, where she enthusiastically serves Apostle Sylvia L. Moore and her church family. She is a prophet, teacher, preacher, and intercessor.

In 2000, she launched In Due Season Publishing Company LLC, which also publishes e-books and children's books. She has been called a purpose-pusher and a midwife to end time scribes. She assists new and seasoned authors in birthing their books by coaching, encouraging and challenging them to leave a legacy in the earth. God has gifted her to connect with the hearts of her God assigned authors and helps them to bring their words to life.

She is also a Poet, and some of her poetry has been recognized by the International Library of Poetry and has been professionally recorded as part of a poetry collection entitled *"The Sound of Poetry."* Her written work has been added in an anthology entitled *"What Tomorrow Holds"* and she was awarded the Editor's Choice Award for Outstanding Achievement in Poetry and the

ENGER LANIER TAYLOR

International Library of Poetry.

Enger has a servant's heart and her desire is to encourage others while they "grow through" their trials while pursuing God's purpose and destiny for their lives. Her ultimate goal is that God get the Glory through all that she does.

She is the daughter of the late Percy Lee Lanier and Mosetta Lanier Woods and has been married to the love of her life, Reuben O. Taylor Sr. for 30 years. They have two adult children (Reuben O. Taylor II, and Austin Percy Taylor) and one granddaughter (Courtlynn Elizabeth Taylor).

www.ingramcontent.com/pod-product-compliance
Lightning Source LLC
Chambersburg PA
CBHW080443110426
42743CB00016B/3265